"Service with Civility"
This book is dedicated to all of those
Shopkeepers, staff and traders who have
Served the people of Thorpe St Andrew.

This book is also dedicated to Christine for her patience and support
and Nick Williams for his belief and support of this project.

Don Laxen (Red) at Beechwood Stores with Snowman in 1981.

Dolly Strangleman and Lucy Waters at J.Waters, 104 Yarmouth Road.

FROM A WAGON TO THE WEB

THE STORY OF THE SHOPS AND TRADES IN THORPE ST ANDREW

1900-2016

Volume one

By Dale Wiseman and Roger Pointer

The authors have made every effort to represent the shops and their owners during the period of time covered. Due to the space and the information available we have had to hand pick those shops that are featured. The authors are grateful to all contributors without whom this varied representation would have been an unrealistic challenge.

Printed by

Gowise Print, Thorpe St Andrew
www.gowise.co.uk

Published by

Copyright © Dale Wiseman and Roger Pointer 2016

Thanks go to Alan Smith, Sue Seymour, Sue Gooch, Thorpe History Group, Diana Mazzoni, Diane Goldsmith, Trevor Fish, Nick Gorvin, Neal Gurney, Beryl Forkes, Harvey Platt, John Moore, Sue Nudd, Barbera Tabor-Ford, Andy and Tony, Vijay Dhalla, Christine Cutting, Nick and Gill Williams, Val and David Warman and all the people of Thorpe who have contributed to this book.

ISBN 978-0-9930518-1-4

Index

An Introduction

THE IDEA FOR THIS PUBLICATION was born out of an interest into how shops and businesses form an important part of the fabric of an area as diverse as Thorpe St Andrew. The story begins in the early 1900s when this area was a village next to Norwich. As the 20th century progressed the village went on to be a Parish and eventually a Town in its own right. This level of growth had to be matched with the demand on types of shops, and the sheer amount of shops. Variety and competition became key words for the then shopkeeper. The Parker family were one such family who were running a large local shop at the start of the twentieth century. This position they would fulfil and hold until the 1960s. Their story and development set the tone for other shops to develop. By the end of World War Two, Thorpe was almost doubled in size, not only with housing stock, but in the number of shops being opened. From grocers to butchers to hardware, people were in the frame to spend.

The 1950s brought about one of the biggest changes that shoppers would ever experience in the shape of self service. This and the arrival of supermarket style shops would change the way we shop for good. Through the thread of this publication we would like to trace the changes, buildings and people who have served this ever developing area. Many local families would go on to become shopkeepers and become important to the community that they served on a daily basis.

The bigger picture is that we are a nation of shopkeepers, but how does this relate to Thorpe St Andrew? As we progress through this period of just over one hundred years we will feature many family names that have provided these shop services. Names like Whittaker, Forke's, and Thurston to mention a few. Their trades and commitment to service become this story. Trades like butchery, baking, sub post-masters and ironmongers to mention a few. We shall also look at the location of these shops. There is a grid map on the index page which will locate these past and present shops. The book will be anchored between the man on his horse on the front cover, Caley Parker, and the modern businessman Neal Gurney who is the reflection of the modern shopkeeper.

A Nation of Shopkeepers

WHEN NAPOLEON DREW HIMSELF UP to full height to deliver a lasting insult to the English, his remark turned out to be memorable enough but not particularly offensive. The English came to adopt the label 'a nation of shopkeepers' with a sense of pride. The phrase can be taken to suggest certain qualities of individuality and independence in the national character, although what Napoleon meant was a nation so preoccupied with commerce would be unfit for war.

Grenville Havenland argues that Napoleon was almost certainly quoting Adam Smith's Wealth of Nations -'To found a great Empire for the sole purpose of reigning up a people of customers may at first sight appear fit only for a nation of shopkeepers; but extremely fit for a nation that is governed by shopkeepers'.

The description of England by Napoleon was intended as an insult, but the English came to adopt the offending title with pride. Throughout the years the English shop has changed and with each generation there are those who regretted that change. In Napoleon's day there was only one type of shop, and that was the small shop. The man who owned it, ran it, and more often than not lived above it. Today the story is different. The small shops may have dwindled in numbers as the retail trade has become progressively dominated by larger stores which carry a broader and sometimes less specialized range of merchandise.

2

SOUTH-WEST

Yarmouth Road to Thorpe Green

PARKERSDASHDENHAMMcCARTHYJOHNSON
FROSTROUTCARVERCLAPHAMMOORE

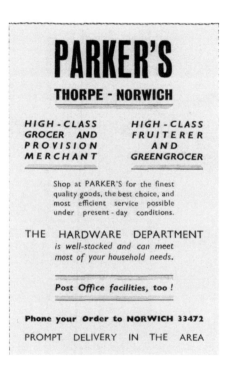

77 Yarmouth Road

James Caley Parker lived at 63 Yarmouth Road, 'Homestead' in 1890. He had two daughters and two sons, Eleanor, Caley and Walter and the youngest Olive. In 1901 Walter took the big step of purchasing 77 Yarmouth Road from Dr. Hill who was the Chief Medical Officer at Thorpe Mental Hospital. In 1901 no. 77 was a double fronted house with an attractive garden at the front which abutted the Yarmouth Road. Walter had big plans and in 1902 he commissioned the large extension that we see the plans for on the next page.

Eleanor (Nellie) was not strong as a girl and in order to give her a comfortable way of earning a living her father James hired a room on the corner of Chapel Lane and Yarmouth Road. This was run as a haberdashery from 1886. In 1890 Eleanor and Walter were also operating a small shop and Post Office between the Buck and Homestead.

The family were able to move into 77 Yarmouth Road by the winter of 1902. The new premises were to be run as a general shop and Post Office. Walter delegated Eleanor and her younger sister Olive to run this new premises as a General Store and a Post Office. Walter and Caley were often to be seen at 77. One of Olive's favorite memories was in 1905 when she was able to skate from Thorpe to Bramerton Woods End on the frozen River Yare. In 1919 Walter moved away from Thorpe and transferred ownership to Nellie. Sometime later their brother Caley moved to 77 and on the death of Nellie in 1930 (aged 63) the property became his. Olive continued to live there and work, till her untimely death on 22 January 1942. Olive was returning from delivering a telegram on her bicycle, when she was knocked down near the Gardens Public House (Thorpe Narrows) by an army ambulance, on an icy road and died. Olive was seventy by this time. The following tribute was written by Rev R. Fielding, Rector in the Parish magazine.

RIP, by Rev. Fielding.

"The sympathy of the whole Parish is with Mr. C. Parker, of the Post Office, in the death of his sister under such tragic circumstances. For many years Miss Parker was a devout and regular worshipper in the Parish Church, and was respected by all, and there are many who knew her. If any consolation is to be got from so sudden and tragic a death, it is that she died immediately and without suffering. May she rest in peace."

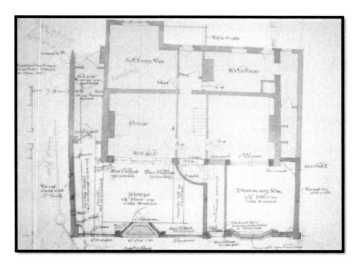

The first drawing is the front elevation for the 1902 extension. These plans were drawn up by Edward Boardman. The second drawing is the ground floor plan. Note where the previous shop in the existing building was. This work was completed in 1902 at a cost of £81.5s.11d.

Caley Stephen Parker was born in 1874 in Norwich. The 1891 census shows him to be a warehouseman clerk, but by 1901 his vocation was as a commercial travellor in drapery. The postcard featured on the next page shows Caley S. Parker in 1908, on his mode of transport for this job. The wagon he is on is purpose built for deliveries and pick-ups. The horse appears to be of fine stock and one can draw a conclusion that there could have been stables to the rear of no. 77 or maybe on Chapel Lane. The reverse of the postcard features a personal message from Caley to a friend Mr. W. The message tells of a wedding which went well. By the time of Olive's death he himself was sixty eight. Two years later Caley made the decision to lease the property and business to his nephew Hugh Caley Parker (b.1907). Hugh and his wife Hilda, and their children Jan and Martin took over the running of the shop. The 1911 census puts Ethel Watson, age 24 at no 77 as a maid/servant (she slept above the kitchen and used the back stairs). Hilda soon noticed that Ethel and Caley were on affectionate terms, something that Caley had been at pains to keep from Olive! In November 1942 they were married by a special licence and went to live on Thunder Lane. After Ethel's death in 1952, Caley moved back to no. 77 until his death in 1955, when the house was willed to Hugh.

Hugh continued to run the shop and Post Office until the late 1950s when he sold the business to Sid Lake. Sid had worked for the family for many years. The Parker family continued to live at 77 for many years. Rosamund was born there in 1949. The family moved out into the county in the early 1970s. However Hugh and Hilda returned to 77 in the early 1980s until their deaths in 1996 and 1992 respectfully.

By the beginning of the twentieth century the general retailer had established himself as an essential element within village life. The village shop had become the focal point of the community, even more than the public house. Parkers shop was in prime position at the heart of the village. The shop became the place where the locals met to exchange news and gossip. Shop hours could be long and tedious with possible opening hours up to 7pm on a Monday and Tuesday and 8.30pm on a Friday and Saturday.

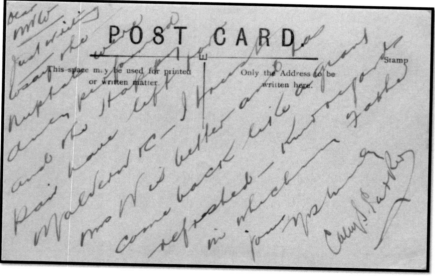

Thorpe Green as it was in 1930.

Parker Stores pictured in the 1940s.

Above we have the headstone for Hugh and Hilda Parker. This is located in the Thorpe St Andrew cemetery and there is a nice nod to their time and dedication to River Green Stores.

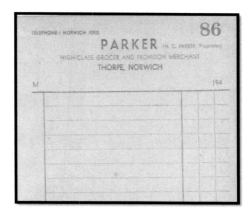

Here is some headed paper from Parkers from the 1940s.

Fond memories of Chapel Lane and its shops, 10/3/94.

From the Press: Karen Etheridge and Annie Ogden

What is in a name? Well, when you live along Rotten Row, quite a lot it seems. Rotten Row is a group of houses at the top of Chapel Lane and at a right angle to the rest. Most of the residents have heard that they live on Rotten Row but firstly do not know what it means or if it is a true name. According to the late Janet Smith the name was registered as a postal address and offered four explanations for the row.

- It could be the route taken by the carts delivering corpses to the church.

- A section of soft earth.

- A slang derivative of the French route Roi or Kings route.

- Where soldiers used to stand to attention during their parade.

All of these suggestions relate to Thorpe St Andrew's Chapel Lane.

The newsagent and post office although not actually on the Lane, have been adopted by the miniature community. For some people the two shops round the corner on Yarmouth Road are a lifeline for people who may not be able to make it to the supermarket. Mike Oliver and Danny Brown who own and run the post office and River green stores believe the relationship between the shops and residents has been a particularly good one. Mike Oliver said "I do a lot of running around, making deliveries and getting anything that someone might need that they cannot get elsewhere or need urgently, as a small shop, if I want to survive then I have to do that. It's not a problem and the customers know that they must use the shop if it is to stay open."

Previous shopkeepers of 73 Yarmouth Road include H. and D. Rout and Peter Dash, both newsagent and general stores. Chris Denham, owner of the neighbouring newsagent, 75 Yarmouth Road, who provides some Chapel Lane homes with their daily read, added "We are not a rural area here but we are still a community and very much rely on the people of Chapel Lane. We have a good relationship with them and I like to think that is because we offer good friendly service".

In October 1995 Mike Oliver closed his business at 77 which allowed Chris Denham the opportunity to extend into 77 and create a Super shop. Chris said "It came to a head when Mike moved his post office into my shop." The Super shop had also undergone extensive improvements and Mr. Denham added: "There is a possibility of future expansion of the post office." Chris has been assisted in this move by wife Carrie and daughter Jo.

This shows the Super Shop as run by Chris Denham at 71-73.

Another business that operated in this area with the most appropriate name was that of Ernest Grief (b.1866). Mr. Grief was an undertaker between the wars. He had previously been a paperhanger and an upholsterer when he lived on City Road, Norwich with his wife Emma. In close proximity to him we also had Philip Buck, the blacksmith.

21 Yarmouth Road

A. & P. McCarthy, Café and Provisions Merchants.

At the Norwich end of Yarmouth Road the first business you would have come across in the 1950s and 60s was Mac's Café. This had previously been the Victoria Tearooms. This establishment was run by Annie McCarthy from around 1948. In 1970 the running of this place was handed over to one of her sons Levi McCarthy, but Annie was still on hand to help out, when needed.

It appears that Levi was a well-known character, being a regular on the doors of several night clubs and music venues in the City. The Café became a favourite for many Norwich fans making their way home after a game. Several would regularly end up at the Café in the early hours of a Sunday morning after watching the Canaries. Do not forget that this is the age before Sky Sports, when Norwich matches would always kick off at 3pm on the Saturday! One of these supporters added "Mac's Café had the best food in England at 2am, problem was every time you nearly got your order a big bloke said it was his - eventually you would eat at 4am".

The EDP reported that the Café also became a meeting place for greasers and skinheads. The paper reports that on 8th February 1971, eight people appeared before magistrates in Norwich after a major disturbance at Mac's Café the weekend before. There had been a fight between the two groups, in which an iron hinge and lumps of building blocks were used. The hinge was allegedly thrown at a Ford Consul which was being driven past the Café by one of the accused.

Local resident Harvey Platt has fond memories of Levi, coming across him in the music scene at the time. He recalls Levi had a familiar saying which he used to describe most situations which was "that's tha gaame" in his broad Norfolk accent. In the days before his death, from a heart attack in 2002, Levi was still a familiar face around Norwich; a big man you could hardly miss in his blue Crombie coat.

The photo above shows the Café before closure.

In an EEN report in December 1976 it was reported that the people of Thorpe have been puzzled by the sudden closure of Mac's Café, on Yarmouth Road. Until recently it was the only all-nighter in the Norwich area. Mrs. Annie McCarthy who lived at the Costessey home of her sister told the reporter that she has decided to sell the business, and it will come up for auction in February. Mrs. McCarthy has run the Café for twenty eight years. Six years ago Mrs. McCarthy gave over the running of the premises to her son Levi, but came in often to help out. "I am not well enough to help out any longer", she said.

97 Yarmouth Road, Parfitt's Sweet Shop

Local resident Sue Seymour remembers this shop being run by two sisters, one slim and one slightly larger, and a brother. Hilda, the slim one, was a great character, she would dance around the shop. This shop sold sweets, basic toys, tinned food and Christmas decorations.

Thorpe between the wars.

TO APPRECIATE THE BIGGEST DEVELOPMENT of housing and population in Thorpe our attention is drawn to the period between the wars. The amount of house building had to be matched by schools, shops and infrastructure. In the Kelly's Trade Directory of 1933 Thorpe Village listed only sixteen shops. In the 1937 edition it listed no fewer than thirty two shops. By 1945 you had the eight precinct areas of shops which all still relevant today. The big change was evident in the amount of shops like the butchers. In 1933 there was one compared to five in 1937. General shops also saw an increase. In 1933 two were listed, in 1937 no fewer than eight shops appeared. Several of the shopkeepers listed in Kelly's Directory during this period we have not been able to locate are as follows:

Kelly's Directory, 1922.

James Goffin, boot seller.

Arthur Watson, shopkeeper.

John Nicolas, boot and shoe repairs.

Kelly's Directory, 1937.

Geo Ransome.

Florence Kelf, shopkeeper.

Harriot Morley, shopkeeper.

Clare Brooks, shopkeeper.

Dorothy Arthurton, newsagent.

By 1937 Thorpe had two post offices to cover an expanding area and population. This period was also one where the shopkeeper became more business-like. The man or woman who ran the corner shop had more control over their shop. A lot of their expertise lay in the ability to procure goods in large quantities from manufacturers, producers and wholesalers at a reasonable price and quality. I get the impression that the Parker family were part of this new breed of shopkeepers.

Reeve and Bury were one of the new fleet of general stores to pop up in this area between the wars. This advert shows the large range of products and also note the writing of their phone number.

J. S. Smith & Sons was another of the new breed of shops, this time on the new Hillcrest Estate. Not quite sure what the line 'just one more customer wanted' means, perhaps there was a prize for the next customer through the door.

16

NORTH-WEST

Plumstead Road East to Hillcrest Road

GOLDSMITHHARDENWEBSTERBINGHAMFISHSMITHGARRETT
LARDERWHITHEADJERMYCLARKEWRIGHTMAZZONIRUDD

17

THE PARADE OF SHOPS AT no.12 to 18 Plumstead Road East has seen many changes over the period since it was first built in the 1940s. One of the earliest shopkeepers at no.18 was D. T. Harden who dealt in high class groceries and provisions. His motto was 'Service with Civility,' you do not hear those words very often these days. The next occupant at 18 was Oliver Goldsmith who was a general grocer and provision merchant. In addition to this he also sold cigarettes and confectionary. Evelyn Goldsmith, his wife, also ran a small shop at no 12, the other end to Oliver.

Alongside them was R. F. Bingham at no.14 who supplied any kind of domestic hardware. As the advert shows, this would cover a vast range from oil to hardboard. The original shop had been run by two older brothers, Russell and Kenneth when they came out of the forces in 1946. They sold a range of hardware goods, radios and cycles. A former regular in the Army, Douglas moved into the business in 1951 and Peter left Jarrolds to join him. The next big change was when the Bingham brothers expanded to become Thorpe Electrical and Cycle and moved in to nos. 12, 14 and 16. This became a small empire where you could purchase almost any household items from a freezer to a paintbrush. Douglas and his brother Peter also stocked a large range of Puch and Raleigh bikes. Unfortunately, by 1989 after forty years their door was locked for the last time, a sad day for the Bingham family. Douglas Bingham said "we couldn't carry on as were any longer. It is a shame and we shall certainly miss everyone."

There was another business that was run behind these shop fronts and that was Geoffrey Spalding who dealt in scrap metal. He was born at the nearest house to this development, no. 20 where his parents William and Alice lived.

The photos on the next page show the buildings that had existed from the 1940s prior to demolition. These buildings did sit about for a short while prior to the eventual demolition as the second photo shows. The area was renamed Bodmin Court, which was named after the Bodmin airplane, which was an experimental British twin-engine biplane bomber of which only two were built by Boulton and Paul at their Mousehold factory in 1924. The new development consists of retail units with residential flats above and behind.

There is another parade of shops at the other end of Plumstead Road East which includes the shops at 140-144, which is now run by Trevor Fish. In 1959 Trevor's dad Victor was running a newsagent at no.140. Victor was assisted by his wife Molly after acquiring the premises from Mr. Buckle who lived and owned this parade of shops. Victor was a butcher after leaving the Army. His initial interest in newspapers was as a newspaper rounds-man in Thorpe for three years. This would have involved the sorting out and distribution of papers on some fifty plus rounds, no mean feat, from the back of a car. By the 1970s he specialized in newspapers, tobacco, toys, wool and was an agent for Air Fix. On his advert he also used the words 'Service and Civility'. Victor would go on to run this business for twenty seven years until his retirement in July 1984. Meanwhile his son Trevor had already acquired a newspaper shop in Sprowston. Trevor had previously been one of those paperboys for his father as well as selling photography equipment. On Victor's retirement Trevor took up the opportunity to be the newsagent at 140 and the Sprowston business was sold. This store has since had the input of the Ideal Store, a few years ago. This store is now a Premier Food and Wine store run by Trevor with the core input of paper deliveries being maintained for as long as possible in the current climate. Opening hours are long including 06:30 to 20:00 hrs on a Saturday. This store is one of ten Premier shops in Norwich and the surrounding areas.

Trevor's son, Alex works full time in the shop, alongside another long standing employee, Janet Kay.

Alongside these shops is the Frying Machine at 156 Furze Road. This used to be the County Stores (Norfolk Ltd). This was a high class greengrocer and followed the latest trend in 1970 of including frozen foods with daily deliveries.

At 144, Arthur Larder M.P.S. who ran a complete Pharmacy service which included cosmetics and baby foods. Arthur was born in Cromer and followed his father Fredrick's footsteps as a chemist. This store later became Larder and Whitehead. The photo on the next page shows a bottle of methylated spirits in an old green glass whisky bottle, which has been issued from Arthur Larder's shop. Below we can see a small bottle of cream issued from this shop. These were in a collection of shoe repairer's tools belonging to Arthur Parker of 52 Spinney Road. Mr. Parker was formerly employed at Haldinsteins and Howlett and White factories from the late 1930s to the 1970s.

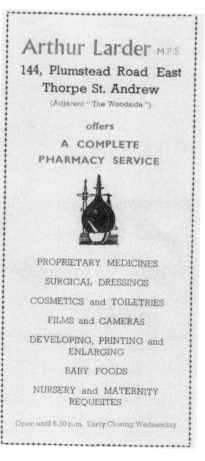

Arthur Larder M.P.S.

144, Plumstead Road East
Thorpe St. Andrew
(Adjacent " The Woodside ")

offers

A COMPLETE
PHARMACY SERVICE

PROPRIETARY MEDICINES

SURGICAL DRESSINGS

COSMETICS and TOILETRIES

FILMS and CAMERAS

DEVELOPING, PRINTING and
ENLARGING

BABY FOODS

NURSERY and MATERNITY
REQUISITES

Open until 6.30 p.m. Early Closing Wednesday

The next group of shops that were part of the building of the 1930s, are on Gordon Avenue/Hillcrest Road. This was part of the new Hillcrest Estate. One of the longest standing shops on here is no. 79 and later 79A. One of its previous occupants was the Osbourne family who ran a Grocers and newsagent. It would later become the Gordon Stores who not only sold high class grocery but also sold diabetic foods and Walls ice cream to name a few. In the late 1960s the proprietor was R. C. Garrett who then sold out to Nello Mazzonni in 1971.

Nello came to Norwich as an Italian prisoner of war. He fell in love with a local girl and decided to settle in the area. For a while he ran a duck farm at Thorpe Abbotts. His daughter Diana fondly remembers the freedom of living out in the country. Diana remembers that her dad started at a small semi house with twelve ducks which ended up being in the hundreds. Nello also ran a fish shop in Bungay and ran that with the family before buying no 79 Gordon Avenue in 1971. Nello died in 1983, but his family decided to carry on with the shop. Diana recalls "he was a well respected gentleman and quite a character, he would often be chatting to someone in English and then just drift off into Italian leaving then partly confused and amused."

Prior to 1995 the shop was split with 79A becoming a newsagent and 79 became various businesses. Life of the newsagent is not always easy when you run a shop as the events of 12th April 1995 proved at these premises. The EDP reported that on the previous day fire ripped through a Norwich babywear shop at 79 Gordon Avenue. Diana Mazzonni only realized she was sitting on top of a blaze when a member of staff started banging furiously on the ceiling. There were waves of black smoke suddenly coming in through the walls of the newsagents. She said "I was talking to a customer and suddenly we both heard this rushing sound and smoke started to come in through the walls. The owner of the shop, Cradles had left the premises a short time prior to this. Sub-Officer Paul Amis of Norfolk Fire Service said "fire fighters battled through the seat of the fire which appeared at the back of the shop."

The family has run the newsagent for many years, Diana says "you get to know the people around here, if you have a chat and a smile then they will come back again." Another point Diana made was that some have become good friends rather than just customers and are very supportive.

Mazzoni's photographed in 2015, all ready for Christmas.

Saturday 27th June 1942.

On a normal Saturday night, alongside an almost full moon, the barrage balloons slowly rose into the sky. The first sign of any activity in the clear sky was the illumination of the parachute-flares north west of the City. This was followed by anti-aircraft activity. The enemy planes penetrated these defences and for the next three-quarters of an hour the City of Norwich was under attack. This early morning raid, estimated to be at 02.05, became the largest fire-bomb raid mounted against East Anglia during the war. An estimated 20,000 incendiaries and some 33 high-explosives bombs were dropped on the City. Among the many areas of damage were the Cathedral, Thorpe Train Station, St Paul's Church and Carrow Abbey. As part of this assult, Mousehold Barracks, Ketts Hill and houses in Thorpe Hamlet were damaged. Two properties on Gordon Avenue took direct hits as the aircraft left the City. One of these was 79 Gordon Avenue. These premises were a provision store, J. S. Smith at the time. As the log shows, the call out happened at 02.40 and was rated as a small fire. Under the leadership of Fireman Betts the damage shown was to the roof and top floor.

This early morning raid proved to be a major hit for the enemy as an estimated 117 private houses were gutted and 246 were damaged. Many offices and shops suffered with 30 totally destroyed and ten others damaged by fire.

There were some other shops on Gordon Avenue which include the following: in 1937 Arnold Rudd ran a butchers, Mrs. Dorothy Arthurton ran a newsagent and J. S Smith was a baker and confectioner at 76 Gordon Avenue, which is now a private house. In the 1950s S. R. Clarke had a general store at 86, again a private property now.

Across the road there used to be two shops and now there is only one at 2 Hillcrest Road. No 4 was sold as a shop and dwelling house for £900.00 in 1945. No 84 Gordon Avenue was also sold in 1945 as a shop and dwelling house for £900.00 alongside no 86 which also sold for £815.00.

The St Williams/ Thunder Lane area has several shops on the corner junction of the two roads mentioned. At 150 St Williams Way now stands Norwich Car Centre. This was previously in the hands of Frank Wright in the 1930s and A. E. Woolsey after him into the 1950s. At 150 now stands The Salon, previously this was a shoe shop under the name of Helena Shoe Stores and at a later stage under Thorpe Shoe and Repair Services belonging to S. Fuller.

At 159 Thunder Lane Percy and Dorothy Howard ran Howards General Store from 1936 through to 1948. This then became a Grocers with Stanley Jermy well into to the 1960s. The shop next door at 161 was a butchers run by Fred Tuddenham. According to trade records this was quite a long standing business in Thorpe.

Under the Rule of Rationing

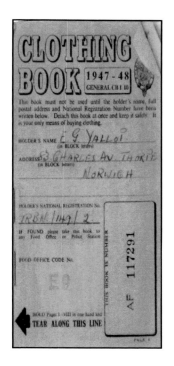

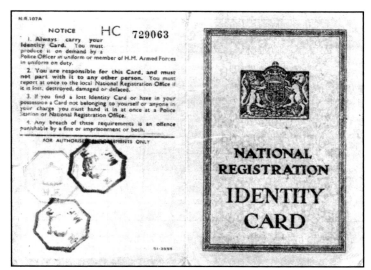

WHEN WE TALK ABOUT THE story of shops it is important that we deal with the idea of rationing, which lasted in different guises, for fifteen years from 1939 through to July 1954. The first product to be rationed was petrol in 1939. Prior to this the United Kingdom had imported twenty million long tons of food per year, including more than 50% of its meat, 70% of its cheese and sugar, 8% of its fruit and about 70% of cereals and fats. In 1939 the civilian population was estimated to be in the region of fifty million.

In January 1940 the real implications of rationing would have been felt in Thorpe Village when bacon, sugar and butter were rationed. The first step towards this was the issue of the National Registration Identity Card. The women had the task of collecting the whole family's birth certificates and taking them to the local church or school. The card pictured on the previous page was issued to Elsie Yallop in 1943, who lived at 83 Charles Avenue. It is probable that her local administration point was the Good Shepherd Church on Thunder Lane. There were two types of ration book issued, the food book and the clothing book. One of the examples shown is the clothing book issued to Elsie Yallop and the food book issued to a youth, D. Wright of Gypsy Close in Norwich.

The grocer and butcher became an important part of the community during these periods, due to the strict guidelines that they had to adhere to. As the photo shows, the books worked on a coupon system. A typical persons weekly ration could well consist of one egg, two ounces each of tea and butter, an ounce of cheese, eight ounces of sugar, four ounces of bacon and four of margarine. Meat was rationed by price rather than weight, and the housewife was more likely to be seen to accept the cheaper cuts with an eye towards value. Interestingly the clothes rationing only lasted till May 1949 due to the difficulty of enforcement. These attempts were defeated by continual massive illegality, including the unofficial trade in loose clothing coupons (many forged) and bulk thefts of unissued clothes ration books.

Records show that one of the toughest years was 1947. In the year of the royal wedding of Princess Elizabeth and the Duke of Edinburgh, the country was in desperate need of cheering up. The winning wartime spirit had been worn down by the lack of everything: food, adequate housing, money and prospects. It appeared that the only thing in abundance were rationing coupons. In 1947 all of the following were restricted; meat, butter, lard, margarine, tea, cheese, sugar, soap, clothing, petrol and sweets.

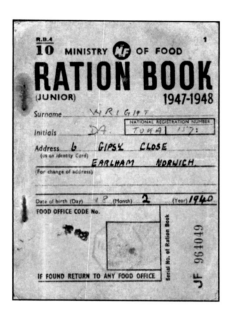

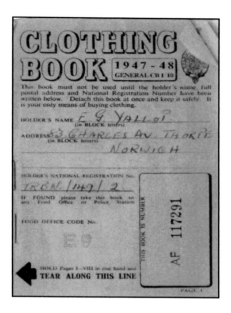

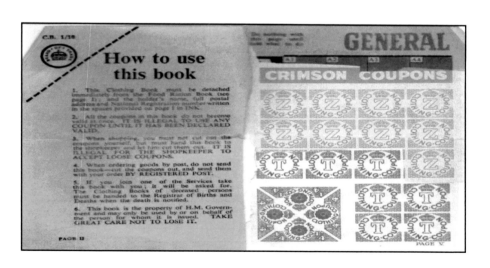

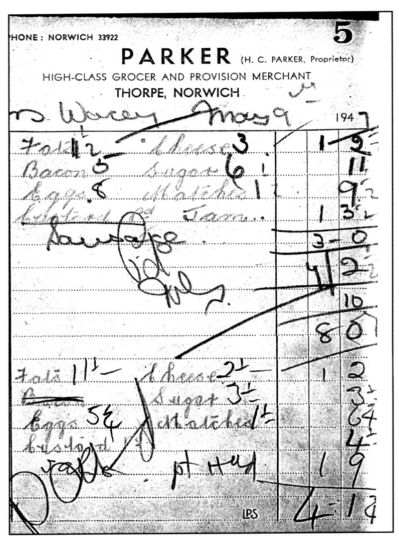

A receipt issued in May 1947, one of the toughest periods, shows some of the above mentioned items.

30

Two adverts that represent Thorpe during the time of rationing. Reeve and Bury have had to stop supplying their famous cooked ham, but they are promising better times ahead.

H. C. Parker are still trading and keeping their service levels as the best. Also they point out that it is better to shop local and save petrol.

Time to Deliver

THE ONLY EXPERIENCE THAT I have had of working in a shop, apart from redecoration work, was as a paperboy. This I carried out from 1976 at Bell's Newsagent in Earlham House on Earlham Road. This was a great experience and I did all three rounds at different times, ending up with a Sunday round. The main problem with the Sunday round was having to do it in two parts, due to the sheer weight of the bag. The role of paperboy or girl is often the first job that a youngster can do, therefore it is a relatively low-standing job with relatively low-pay. This should not take away the effectiveness of the job and some Christmas's were very fruitful as far as tips were concerned. One of my strongest memories was of Wednesday August 17th 1977. That very day, when sorting out the papers, I saw the headlines on the front of the Sun "King Elvis Dead". Being from a family where music was always around I only had one thought, I have got to tell someone this important news. In my haste I went straight home and told Mum and Dad, at the time I was only beginning to understand the magnitude of this story, that had happened over night, in America. Luckily I was able to get back on track and deliver my sixty papers.

The role of the paper boy/girl has always been an important first job for many of us youngsters. The following two stories are from features that appeared in the local press in 1994. One of Chris Denham's paperboys in 1994 was a 16-year-old, Chris Smith. Chris was a sixth-former at Thorpe St Andrew School and some days he managed to fit in a 15-hour day. His day starts at 6.30am when he gets up for his paper round, then it is off to school. After school on Tuesdays and Thursdays as well as Saturdays he works in the Castle Mall in the Disney Shop, sometimes till 9pm. Chris added " On my round I don't get to see many people, but the other day, someone did come out to meet me and gave me a bar of chocolate."

Another paper boy from Chris Denham's shop made the news in the same year. Eastern Evening delivery boy Jonathan Perks has been rewarded for his quick thinking which may have saved an elderly woman's life. In February 1994 Jonathan climbed into the women's garden in Thorpe St Andrew and found her lying there, after he had heard faint cries for help. When he could not find her husband, he rushed to a neighbour's house to call an ambulance. Jonathan only heard Mrs. Burgess because he had forgotten his Walkman this day. He vows not to wear it again on his round. Then the 14 year-old Thorpe St Andrew School pupil was rewarded for his good deed with a certificate of merit and a cheque. "I am putting the money towards a drum kit - I am learning to play drums at the moment," said Jonathan, who likes all sorts of music, especially heavy metal. Mrs. Burgess was taken to hospital where her condition was described as satisfactory. Proud mum Norma said

"He didn't walk away. He did everything right. I think he was wonderful."

Newsagent Chris Denham nominated Jonathan for the national Carl Bridgewater Award, said he was very proud of his young employer. "It's smashing. He did a good job and knew just what to do," he said. The award was named after the 13 year-old Carl Bridgewater who was murdered while doing his paper round in the West Midlands in 1978. It rewards outstanding behaviour by delivery boys or girls.

As previously mentioned, not all rounds were directly dealt with from a shop, as was the role that Victor Fish played as a newspaper rounds-man in the late 1950s. Trevor Fish recalls the importance of this delivery service. Trevor stills holds on to this core part of the business of being a newsagent but is very much aware that the format of paper deliveries is slowly disappearing due to habit changes of readership, availability of papers in most other shops and the emergence of the papers online. Trevor says, "the larger companies see delivery as preventing the customer from visiting the shop, but there is an importance in the contact with the customer either in the shop or through the delivery process".

Other paperboys/girls who have worked for Trevor include Laura Wiseman, Jack Wiseman and Roger Pointer amongst many others.

Fish News, Plumstead Road East.

34

NORTH-EAST

Thunder Lane to Pound lane

LAXENSTHURSTONBOBBIEBURRWEBSTERREEVE&BURYWEBB
CUNNINGHAMTABOR-FORDDIANECULYERTUDDENHAMCOX

Beechwood Stores, 204 Thunder Lane.

'Bench marks a family business.'

EDP, 7/12/1988.

THORPE WAS STILL A SLEEPY VILLAGE when Cyril Clarke returned from India after the last war. Times have changed and the area has expanded dramatically. But the greengrocer's which Cyril's family bought as a family business in 1848 is still there. Now his family have banded together to dedicate a bench to his memory and that of his son-in-law Donald Laxen who ran the Woodside Stores following Cyril's retirement.

Cyril, served with the Royal Norfolk's in India during the War and returned to this country with his wife Maude and three teenage daughters. They settled into Woodside Stores which they ran until the early 1970s when Donald and their daughter Jean took over. They in turn sold the business which had expanded to include a fish and chip shop two years ago.

The Laxens' son Richard decided to organize the family's tribute to his father and grandfather to keep the link with their "home" village with the help of the local parish council. "They saw Thorpe grow and were part and parcel of the area. Obviously, as time has gone on everyone has moved away or died," says Richard, 36, who now lives in Old Catton and works as a credit controller at Sedgewicks.

"We thought a bench would be a nice gesture, especially as my father and grandfather were so well-liked locally", he added. Present at the unveiling of the bench were April Abel, her daughter Laura, Jean Laxen, Jane Laxen-Creed, Richard Laxen, Canon Brian Pearson and district councilor John Lee.

Maud and Cyril Clarke with Thunder Lane garage in the background.

Donald Laxen and snowy friend pictured outside the store in 1981.

EDP, 5/5//69

A. G. Thurston, 9 The Ring Road.

There has been no eight hour day for Mr. A. G. Thurston these past thirty five years. Regularly, except when he was in the army during the war, he has got up at six in the morning, and it is usually been some twelve or fourteen hours later that he has finally finished his day. But all that changed as from Saturday, Mr. Thurston handed over his fish, fruit and vegetable shop in Thorpe. With his wife and his daughter Hilary, who both help in the shop, he is to retire to Acle. Among the hundreds of Thorpe people who will miss Thurston's will be the old age pensioners, for though he modestly kept quiet about this, he always made a point of "seeing pensioners right"- which means that he charged them less than ruling prices, and often as little as cost price. He also gained a reputation of sending a basket of fruit to any of his friends when they were in hospital.

Mr. Thurston did much of his own buying of fruit, vegetables and fish and he also prepared his own fish for sale. When the shop closed he would set up for the next day. He also cured his own bloaters, and for many years after he came here from Dereham Road, where he had a shop previously, there were open fields around his shop with cows and horses in them. "The roads you see now were just lanes". The Thurston's also kept geese in the early days. Mr. C. Butler became the new owner and was going to carry on the same business model set forward by the Thurston's over the last thirty five years.

37

Just along from this shop is 2 Thorpe Avenue. This shop is currently a charity shop but has had many uses over the years. In 1937 this shop was a grocers under the banner of Reeve and Bury. Leslie Bury (b.1908) and Walter Reeve ran this shop as well as owning the property of 1 Spinney Road.

REEVE & BURY,

Thorpe Avenue Stores, Thunder Lane

THORPE ST. ANDREW

TEL: THORPE DOUBLE THREE.

▼

Have full and comprehensive Stocks of

Groceries, Provisions, Confectionery, Tobaccos

and Cigarettes, Patent Medicines, &c.

We specialize in Bacon, Hams (Own Cooking) and Butter.

Allow us to demonstrate our desire to be of service, no order considered too small.

WE CAN DELIVER YOUR MORNING PAPERS EARLY

ICES. PASTRIES. MINERALS.

It then became a family butchers with Fred Cunningham selling high class meats including rabbits and poultry. This premises would later be an electrical shop before being an Estate Agents Office. Reeve and Bury also ran a general store from the Beechwood Stores premises.

Another shop that has been operating since the housing boom is 1 Spinney Road. James Burr (b.1905) and his wife, Daisy, were the first occupants of this address. They opened up a ladies hair stylist and children's hairdresser under the banner of Bobbie Burr. This shop is still a hairdressers today under the banner of Nicol's. The building was bought by Leslie and Audrey Bury in 1952. Leslie and Walter Reeve also ran Bury and Reeve General Store on Thorpe Avenue for many years.

JANE ELLIS *Hair Fashions*
(formerly Bury's)
1 SPINNEY ROAD - THORPE - Norwich
A versatile staff trained in modern and standard hair-dressing.
Trained not only to style your hair to suit your individuality,
but to cut, colour and perm.
Shampoo and Set 9/6 - - - - **Perms from £1/10/0**
Old Age Pensioners on Monday only at Reduced Rates
OPEN ALL WEEK, except Tuesday—Late night, Thursday
Open all day Saturday
For your appointment ring Norwich 33456

This advert dates back to 1970 and puts Jane Ellis at No 1 Spinney Road. As the advert shows this took over from Bury's as mentioned above.

Don Laxen, Beechwood Stores, September 1978

An extension was added to no 1 in the 1950s and this became 1A. This was to be a florist for Constance Webster. Constance served her time working for Stevenson's the florists before opening her own shop. This shop is still trading under this name and has been run by Barbara Tabor-Ford, since 1978. Mrs. Ford started as a delivery driver with Constance and then fully qualified as a florist before running the place for the last thirty seven years. One memory that Barbara recalls was a phone order she received from the Royal Household in 1980. The call came from London to supply and deliver nine yellow roses to the Ingram Ward at the Norfolk and Norwich Hospital for a Mrs. Lloyd. The instructions for the card, to go with the roses, were from Queen Elizabeth II to her Sandringham Secretary, Mrs. Lloyd. When the cheque arrived, pictured below, Barbara decided to keep it as a memento rather than cash it. The matter was forgotten until the Privy Purse Office called, six months later, and said that their accounts did not add up because the cheque had not been cashed. A second cheque was issued with strict instructions that this had to be cashed within ten days of receiving it and no more would be said.

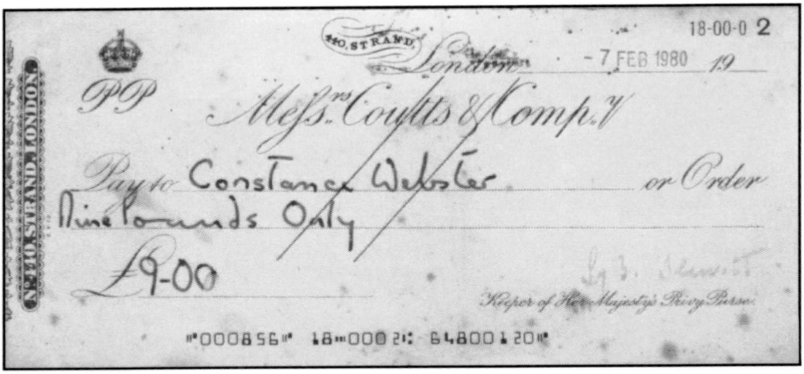

Constance Webster's in 2016, all ready for Valentine's Day. Nicol's hairdressers next door where Bobbie Burr started out.

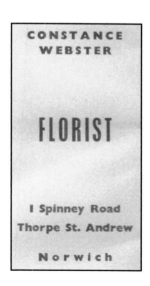

The South Hill parade of shops is another area of many changes. The main parade evolves around two or three larger shop premises and four smaller shop spaces. This appears to have been the rule of thumb since these buildings were completed in the 1940s. One of the earliest shops was at no 52 which was a general store run by the Culyer family. This shop would sell almost any items even including DIY products like paint. Within this shop a name mentioned to me was a Mr. and Mrs. Cox, who apparently were specialists in cutting and selling the best ham and bacons. There is a possibility that they moved over to the shop across the road at a later stage.

Next to this at 52A was first a wool shop and then South Hill News. This is now a beauty and holistic salon. Next to this is Hair by Diane at 52B. The previous ownership of this appears to have been Mr. B. Webb who was a gents hairdressers and then Norma's hair stylist prior to Joan Johnson running a ladies hair salon. In 1980 Diane, with the help of her father, Sidney Stimpson was able to run her own salon after learning the trade at Christine's on Salhouse Road. Diane left school with the vision of being a hairdresser or an actress. Having the opportunity to run her own place has been fulfilling for her and Diane has been, and still is, actively involved in amateur dramatics through several groups including Thorpe Players and Rackheath Players. Diane has experienced seeing many changes in the use of hair products and the competition from other shops. Diane says "one of the reasons for her business still trading is her good staff, which in turns creates a good team". The staff that Diane is referring to are Julie Stevenson and Zoey Faircloth who have been involved in the salon for many years. Diane added "several of our customers are unable to make their way to the shop, so myself or Julie jump in our cars and do a pick up and drop off service". Of their customer base at least twenty five per cent take up this offer. My impression of the salon was as a community hub. This is reinforced by the many charity events that are organized over the course of the year within this shop.

Diane is pictured above with her regular staff, Zoey Faircloth and Julie Stevenson outside her shop.

This area of shops has seen much variety over the years including Mr. Palmer the butcher and George Wright who ran a fruit and hardware shop for many years. This area has also seen a launderette, beauty and holistic, a sweet shop, a wool shop and several gents and ladies hairdressers. Today we have a Londis, a café and a large kitchen shop.

Castons Builders on Belmore Road

43

The "Belmore Business Centre" at 4-6 Belmore Road makes use of the building yard originally owned by the Caston family. Castons had their building offices there from the 1940s.

The current owners of the yard are Ken and Joyce Gorvin, founders of Gowise Print which has traded from this location since inception in 1983. Their son, Nick Gorvin, joined Gowise in 1991 ensuring the company continues as another long established family business in Thorpe St Andrew.

The yard now provides an ideal out of the city trading area for a number of diverse, small businesses. The mainly residential area sets the Belmore Business Centre apart from traditional trading estates and the units are much sought after.

As well as Gowise Print, the Belmore Business Centre is home to a number of other local business:

Polysyne (Norwich), a damp proofing and timber treatment company.

The yard is a base for two prominent Norfolk Catering companies; South Hill Catering who have been providing high quality catering to Norwich, Norfolk and East Anglia for over 20 years and also the Fired Up Food Company.

Healing Naturally Limited, who provide nutritional supplements throughout Europe with a strong web presence.

Accountancy Plus & Payroll People occupy a unique self contained detached office at the back of the yard which was purpose-built by Mr and Mrs Gorvin to replace an old green tin shack which used to stand there.

The photograph above is of the yard back in the early 1980's showing the old green shack at the rear. The shack was a 'starter' home to fledgling company Gowise Print when it all began for them in 1983.

In those days, the larger building to the right was occupied by Belmore Supplies, a builders' merchants. At the time it changed hands the yard was still registered as a builder's yard but the new owners applied for change of use to 'Office and Light Industrial', much to the delight of the Town Council.

The row of mature beech trees that shade the buildings on the south side of the yard now have protected status.

This advert dates back to 1910 and shows the large range of products that William Frost was selling from his premise on Yarmouth Road, on the site of the Buck public house, car park today.

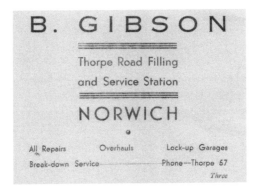

B. Gibson - Thorpe Road.

Forecourt Attendant to Self Service

OVER THE COURSE OF THE century featured in this book, there have been many garages dotted around Thorpe St Andrew from the small one pump unit of William. J. Frost to the pumps of the bigger supermarkets and the oil companies. William Frost was probably the first garage in Thorpe, and his business was situated on what is now the car park of the Buck Inn on Yarmouth Road. It appears that he started out his business of a cycle and motor engineer in the 1920s after moving to Thorpe from Gt Yarmouth. He advertised as an agent for "Fleet" cycles as well as an agent for "Pratts" and "Shell's" motor spirit. This business then developed to sell Esso petrol as in the picture on the previous page. It is thought that by 1961 the pub needed the space for their car park and bought out the business.

This photo, from 1930, shows Frost Repairs as you approach from Norwich City Centre.

During the 1980s and 90s there was another garage on Yarmouth Road, Circle Filling Station which was facing up to the stiff competition of the new supermarkets. John Williams bought the Q8 service station in 1995, but has finally admitted defeat in his David and Goliath battle and is to concentrate on car sales instead. "We can no longer take the pressure," said Mr. Williams, who is making four people redundant. "It is a combination of the supermarkets and the price war started by ESSO. In the end we just cannot compete." His forecourt prices dropped to 62.9p a litre of unleaded and 67.9p a litre for four star. But companies like ESSO, BP and Sainsbury's on Pound Lane, are selling at around 59.9p for unleaded and 65.9p for four star. Mr. Williams said all the independents are suffering. Price wars for two or three months I can cope with, but this has been going on for nearly two years." It is so long to keep up with the big boys. The future for us independents is bleak". Since ESSO launched its Price Watch in March 1996 about 4000 independent garages, many in rural areas have closed. A spokesperson for Sainsbury said "We do aim to offer the most competitive petrol prices but it is a tricky area and we are sympathetic. We do not sell petrol at a loss, it has to pay its way. It is not our aim to close down competitors, but it is a highly competitive market and unfortunately independents are finding it difficult."

In 1938 Caston and Sons, the local builders, built Thorpe Motor Company on the corner of Thunder Lane and Plumstead Road East, which later became Thunder Lane Garage. The idea was that the garage was purpose built for Robert Caston's son Cyril. Sadly Cyril did not return from the war. On 1 January 1953 Frank Batch, who had recently left the Royal Navy, joined Robert Caston in the garage business. In 1957 their garage became Thunder Lane Garage Ltd. This garage has seen many changes over this long period of time as the photo next page shows. It was not sure why the gentlemen were having to fill so many cans at once. One of the biggest changes for this business has been from an attendant filling up your car to the self service of today. As the bill on the next page shows the Batch and Caston families have remained totally involved up to today where Roger Batch and Paul Caston, the sons of Frank and Robert, still run the property. This, alongside the Fish family, makes these two among the longest family run businesses in Thorpe today.

THUNDER LANE GARAGE LTD.

MOTOR ENGINEERS

Directors:
F. L. BATCH
R. CASTON
E. CASTON
M. E. BATCH
R. M. BATCH

THUNDER LANE :: NORWICH

Telephone 33848

M The Secretary, Thorpe Parish Council,   30th April,   1973
          10, Pilling Road, Norwich.

26th March, 1973.	To supplying	6 Gallons	Petrol	£2. 08
	"	5 "	Paraffin	. 65
	"	1 "	Oil	75
				£3. 48

50

This garage was on the Yarmouth Road, opposite the Town House. As the picture shows, Shell were one of the oil companies that owned this unit. I always thought this was a good location for this business with the openness of the road and its sweeping forecourt.

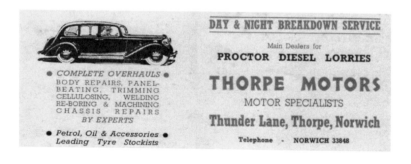

SOUTH-EAST

Thunder Lane to Yarmouth Road

HOWARDSFORKESREAD&SONSWHITTAKERTHORPEBUTCHERSWATERS
SENDALLSPRINGALLPOSTOFFICEDUNHAMSPARKESNUDD

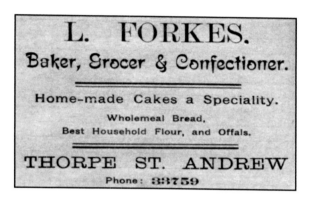

ANOTHER IMPORTANT LONG STANDING BUSINESS just down the road from Parkers store was located at 104 -108 Yarmouth Road. This was the location for a butchers and poultry shop for around eighty years. Electoral records show that J. Waters was a pork butcher and poulterer in 1888 at no 104 Yarmouth Road. This shop was run by Dolly Strangleman, alongside John and Lucy Waters for the period up to 1926. When Bertie Whittaker (1894-1975) bought and extended 104 to include 106 and 108, this then became a site of 0.6 acres. There were various garages, outbuildings and a cottage to the rear. Also there were livestock pens, pig sties, a barn and a slaughterhouse.

The Victorian butchery trade was dominated by men who bought on the hoof, killing and dressing their own meat. Many had market stalls in the bigger cities, but for places like Thorpe fixed shop premises were the answer. The 1870s saw the arrival of live North American cattle which, like European stock, had to be slaughtered at the point of entry within ten days to prevent possible spread of disease. By 1914, 60% of these imports were reported to be pig meat, much of which was cured bacon or ham. These were sold as 'provisions' through grocers' stores such as Parkers and by specialist pork butchers, which J. Waters was. This was the case up until the 1930s for places such as Newcastle and Norwich who saw little or no Argentinian beef. Bertie and wife Hilda (1894-1980) had previously had a butchers shop at 49A Hardy Road in Thorpe Hamlet in 1918. When Bertie return from service in France in the Norfolk Yeomanry, they were able to purchase the properties on Yarmouth Road. They would also go on to have a second shop at 14 Anchor Street in Pockthorpe in the 1950s. Bertie continued to run the shop at Hardy Road until it was taken over by Harry Utting in 1937, alongside his wife Phyllis, who was the only daughter of the Whittakers. In 1939 the Hardy Road shop moved to 93-95 Carrow Road.

This advert is from 1939.

B H WHITTAKER OUTSIDE 104 YARMOUTH ROAD - CIRCA 1970

Hilda Whittaker in full flow.

At 92 Yarmouth Road, Nora and Lawrie Howard ran the ever popular Howard's Bakery. These premises have now been converted back to a house. Nora was born in 1917 in Pulham St Mary, Norfolk. Local resident Oliver Rowe wrote this article in the Beacon in 2005 in tribute to Nora Howard. Nora was orphaned by the age of twenty and, along with her brother Ted, moved to Hall Road with their auntie. Nora went on to have two jobs, one at Butchers, the drapers in Norwich and another at Caribonum, the stationers. Nora enjoyed travelling all over Norfolk with her work. Nora married Lawrie in 1940 and they went into business together. The couple's bakery provided delivery jobs to many teenagers such as the children of Dr Hilton, of Larchwood. Dr. Hilton had a surgery near the Roxley and was much respected by Nora.

Nora and Lawrie had very little time off. Their working day began in the small hours to provide bread for breakfasts and the shop remained open until early evening. Within the shop they had big brick ovens which were heated by an elaborate oil fired blow torch. They also had a large dough mixer which by the time they retired was getting a bit outdated. The bakery closed in 1981 and the shop was mothballed. The couple carried on living at the property in their rooms behind the shop. Lawrie passed away in February 1986 and Nora died in November 2005. Local and loyal friends celebrated the lives of a very popular couple.

92 Yarmouth Road and Nora Howard, left, with her friend Muriel Ames.

Next door was the Forkes shop at no 94. Leonard (b. 1891) and wife Annie ran a baker, grocer and confectioner shop. They were trading from this shop from at least 1922 along with their three children. Leonard was trained as a blacksmith as his father Frederick had a blacksmith shop in Attleborough. Leonard and Annie Crane were married in 1915 in the county of Mitford. His son Richard would end up working in the business with the help of sisters Molly and Betty. Richard, better known as Dick married Beryl in 1944. Beryl would then go on to be an important part of the shop. Beryl would get involved with the regular deliveries and helping out in the shop. Beryl said "life was never dull and the hours could be long". Beryl can remember one busy winter when they delivered on Christmas Day. Beryl also recalls how her father in law Leonard was able to buy the shop in the first place. She recalls "Leonard went to Canada with two of his sisters, they stayed and he came back with the funds to purchase the shop and house at 94 from a Miss Clarke.

As well as family members, George Rice worked for the business for thirty seven years. He was involved with deliveries and the making of wedding cakes and is pictured below.

Beryl recalls "times were tough with the change to convenience shopping, including the introduction of sliced bread by Betabake" Dick eventually stocked and delivered sliced bread but did not eat it. George did carry on making cakes after the shop closed and went to work at St Andrews Hospital until retirement.

The photo below, shows most of the Forkes family at their annual dinner. Annie Forkes is second left, George, fourth right, and next to him Beryl and Dick. These functions at the Aylsham Road Rooms are fondly remembered by Beryl.

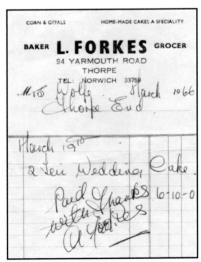

This is what a wedding cake would have cost in 1966.

These photos show Dick's sisters, Molly and Betty at the time of the closure of the Forkes shop.

Just along the road at 156 Yarmouth Road, is another longstanding business. Thorpe Butchers is run by two brothers Andy and Tony. This is a modern high class butchers with a five star Hygiene Rating, which has recently undergone an extensive refit. The business was first established in 1925 and the current pair have been here for over thirty years. The brothers have extensive experience and an excellent long term reputation. Like a lot of smaller shops the business was affected when the supermarket moved it, possibly losing up to 50% of their existing trade. The brothers came through this by turning to outside catering. This has proved successful and they now see this as part of their core business. The refurbished van below was used for promotion at this time of change. The two brothers are pictured below at Great Grove Farm. The earliest recorded shopkeeper for 156 is Thomas Sendall who ran a butchers shop from 1933. Another butcher at this address was E. W. Standen.

Next door to Andy and Tony at 158 is the post office run by Vijay Dhalla. The first registered shop here was that of William Springall with his wife Louisa who ran a grocery and provisions store from 1937. They also sold drapery and tobacco. In the 1950s R. M. Nudd ran a general store from 158.

The next business was Read and Sons and was based at 152 Yarmouth Road. The earliest knowledge of this firm is from 1933. It looks likely that Mr. Read was William Read of Brooklyn Terrace in Thorpe, who was a plumber and decorator. It appears that he carried out building working at Thorpe Asylum which developed into a building business. This then developed into a funeral business as well. He was then joined by Albert Wilkinson who would go on to run this business. Albert was born in 1898 and lived at 33 Yarmouth Road with his wife Alma. They then moved to 152 Yarmouth Road where they ran this multi-purpose shop. Family member Sue Gooch remembers that there was a Chapel of Rest to the rear of this property. Also a workshop which was accessed from the small lane running at the back of Bungalow Lane behind the terraces, coming up near the chip shop. Albert Wilkinson was the funeral director and made the coffins in the work shop. Albert's son Derrick became part of the business and when Albert died in 1954 it appears that Derrick took over the business. Derrick is pictured below with his collegue Ted Weeds at the back of 152 with the works van (KVF 392) in the 1960s.

FUNERAL DIRECTORS
A Complete Funeral Service   Phone Norwich 33973
                                         or 35870
READ & SONS
(Established over 50 years)
Funerals Completely Furnished
Cremations Arranged
Private Chapel of Rest

152 YARMOUTH ROAD
Thorpe St. Andrew, Norwich, NOR 46T

Funerals and Cremations arranged and conducted under the personal
supervision of Mr. D. Wilkinson

This headed bill from 1930 shows the extent of the kind of services that Read and Sons could provide. It is interesting to note the reference to Whitlingham Station in the top right hand corner.

This family photo L to R shows Albert Wilkinson, Derrick Wilkinson, Ted Weeds and his father Billy Weeds all ready for a days work. This firm also carried out many council contracts for Blofield and Flegg Council and were responsible for supplying the posts and the painting of the new street signs in 1939, for all the new builds in Thorpe.

Here are four photos taken during the year of the Queen's Coronation in 1953.

Top left, Dunhams Post Office at 186 Yarmouth Road. Top right, Inside of Parkes Fish Store. Bottom, the outside of Parkes Fish at 188 Yarmouth Road.

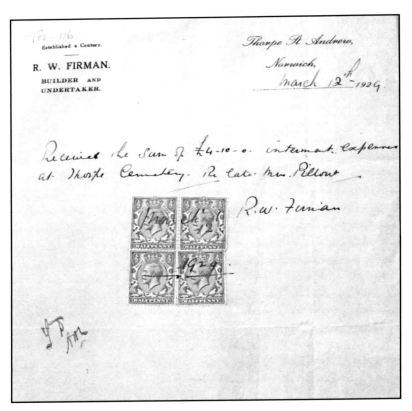

R. W. Firman was in business from the 1920s and was trading very similar to Read and Sons.

The Day the Supermarket arrived in Town

ON TUESDAY 3RD OCTOBER 1989 the new Sainsbury Superstore was opened at Pound Lane. In the advert carried in the local press the company advertised 470 parking spaces, 34 checkouts, clothing, a Pharmacy and many more convenience products. This was not the first convenience store. Some fifteen years previous to this a convenience store had opened at locations like 159 Thunder Lane. The shopkeeper here, Ricky Chung, spent £40,000 on refurbishing this store. He said "It has a completely new look and colour scheme and a much larger door for mums with prams or pushchairs". Among the products was an off licence, a wide range of frozen foods and a fully computerized newspaper system. This store was also open 6am to 8pm.

By the 1980s the idea of superstores was not a new idea. The first blow to the independents was the advent of the multiple chains. One of the first was the Co-operative Movement, an unconventional organization which was a difficult target for local shopkeepers as it was technically owned by the local community - the very people whose custom they were competing for. Entrepreneurs behind firms like Lipton's, Boots and W.H. Smith soon saw that if they could create their own multiple chains they could have the same bulk-buying power and give the personal service of their local rivals.

Prior to the above, the first major onslaught on the corner shop came in the early 1950s, when Britain was still in the grip of post-war austerity. The grocery chains decided to save even more money on staff by importing the self-service ideas from America, Supermarkets had arrived. Although they were eventually to be the deathknell of many a local grocer, the British public's response to supermarkets was not enthusiastic. Some were embarrassed because the wire baskets exposed to everyone's gaze how little they might be buying. Others resented the lack of chat with the salesperson. A few felt that as a Co-op customer it was not their job to be taking goods off the shelves and carrying them around the shop.

Sorting out the mail in the drawing room at 77 Yarmouth Road. To the left is the door into the kitchen. Olive Parker is third from left and Caley Parker is fourth from right. This photo is from the 1930s.

It's in the Post

Post Offices hold a special place in the hearts and minds of the British people. They are frequently places of trust, and the sub-postmaster or sub-postmistress is often held in high regard within the local community. Thorpe is no different, and has a rich history of post offices.

The first recorded sub-postmaster for Thorpe Village was William Plow (b.1781) in 1854, who operated from Thorpe Turnpike Road alongside his shoe repair shop. The next receiver was Daniel Todd in 1872. He was operating from the corner of Chapel Lane and Yarmouth Road. Daniel Todd was born in 1819 and was a woodman as well as a receiver of the post. Records show that his letters would arrive by mail cart from Norwich at 6.30am and had to be dispatched by 6.15pm. The next master was Mr. W. H. Parker in 1883. His letters would arrive at 4.15am and 3.45pm and were to be dispatched by 12 noon and 6.15pm via Norwich.

Frederick Waller Noble was the next sub-postmaster and he was in position from 1886 to 1896. Frederick was born in Norwich in 1853 and had ten children. Frederick's fifth son, Henry, was born in one of the rooms above the post office. He wondered how many of his brothers and sisters were born there. Henry remembers Harts boat yard across the river. Henry recalls that his grandmother got his father the job at the post office, because she was a cleaner to Mr. Winch, who was the post-master of Norwich. Frederick was a carriage builder and worked for his father who had a coach builders shop in Norwich. This firm also built horse drawn vans for the post office.

Now it was the turn of the Parker family to look after the post. In 1896 Walter James Parker took over the reins. In the 1901 census Walter is listed as a grocer, draper and sub postmaster. His wife Eleanor was a sub postmistress. Letters would arrive by mail carts at 4.30am and by foot messenger at 3.30pm. These would then be dispatched by 12.20, 6.10pm and 7.55pm. The wall letter box would be emptied at 12.25, 6.15pm and 8.50pm. By 1908 after the major new extension at 77 Yarmouth Road, there were five wall letter boxes in Thorpe. These were at Sunnyhill, the cemetery wall, at the Asylum, Plumstead Road and on Yarmouth Road.

In 1930 Walter passed over the post office to his children, Caley and Olive. These years between the wars were to prove a time of change for the post. The post-war coalition government abolished the penny post, for the first time since 1840. All letters under 4oz now cost $1\frac{1}{2}$d, later rising to 2d in 1920. Telegram charges rose from 6d to 9d for twelve words. These changes allowed the post office to compete in the competitive marketplace. Interestingly, in contrast to the rationing happening in this country, the post office was running several National Savings Schemes. These were seen as a way of people 'saving their way to Victory'. Another slogan was 'Save by lending and lend by saving'. Employers were encouraged to buy Certificates in advance for resale to their employees by instalments or outright.

At the same time a second post office had sprung up at 140 Thunder Lane. The sub-postmaster this time was Percy Langley. He was also combining the post with that of a general store.

SPINNEY STORES
(P. LANGLEY)

Thunder Lane Post Office
THORPE

❦ GROCERY ❦
CONFECTIONERY
AND TOBACCO

Cooked Meats, etc.   Orders Delivered Daily
Telephone———THORPE 17

Again this store was on the cusp of the massive build of the new Spinney Estate. At around the same time another post office was to open at 186 Yarmouth Road. The first sub-post master here was Russell Dunham (b.1903) assisted by his wife Hattie in 1939. The post office moved along to 158 Yarmouth Road and a Mr. Springhall ran this shop prior to Robert and Olive Nudd, who arrived in 1957. When they were sorting out this property they came across tins of sausages in the shed, left over from World War II, maybe leftovers from the days of rationing. Robert Nudd worked in the construction industry until they ventured into the shop at 158. Olive ran the post office and Robert the general store. Daughter-in-law Jan states that the character of Arkwright by Ronnie Barker could well have been based on Robert Nudd. He had the gift of teasing and tempting the customer to purchase items they did not come in to the shop for. Robert bought fruit and veg from Harford Bridge Market and offered a local delivery service to include holiday makers at Maiden Craft at Bungalow Lane. This business was owned by Jan's father and uncle, Bill and Jack Jenner. Olive was assisted by June Armstrong in the shop. Everybody knew everybody else in that area of Thorpe and all took part in the Green Shield stamp scheme. Jan remembers the effect and fuss that Sunday opening had with the local authorities. As a footnote Jack Jenner sold fruit and veg in Thorpe from a van for several years.

The present Yarmouth Road post office is still at 158 and has been run by Vijay Dhalla for the last 30 years. Vijay says "there are two important points to remember when you run a shop, they are service and customer base". These are the key components to running a shop and post office over the period of upheaval and transition that Mr. and Mrs. Dhalla have experienced in their busy shop on an even busier main road.

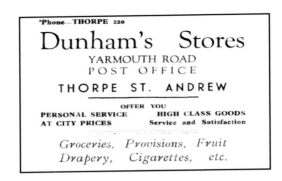

'Phone—THORPE 220

Dunham's Stores

YARMOUTH ROAD
POST OFFICE

THORPE ST. ANDREW

OFFER YOU

PERSONAL SERVICE   HIGH CLASS GOODS
AT CITY PRICES   Service and Satisfaction

Groceries, Provisions, Fruit
Drapery, Cigarettes, etc.

During the 1950s Norwich and surrounding areas became the pioneers of the machine sorting age. In 1959 the first public code was introduced in Norwich. This did not prove too successful at first. Senders only put codes on fewer than half of their letters. Doubts were raised in some quarters about the virtues of extending public coding to the entire country. Advertisements were put out in 1962 to encourage the people of Norwich to use the post code. It was decided in 1965 to proceed with a revised version of the 'alpha-numeric' codes that were used in Norwich. I am sure this idea must have seemed a one dimensional idea at the time, but as we have seen with the technology of the Sat-Nav, the post code is probably used more now than it ever has been.

S. A. Lake, Yarmouth Road. Receipt - 1960.

This is one of the posters used in and around Norwich to encourage the locals to use the new postcode in 1962.

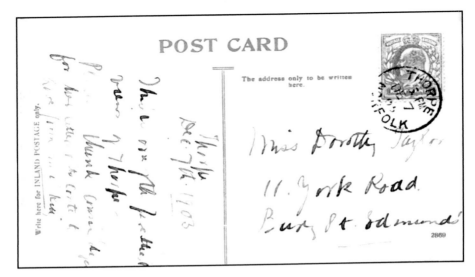

POST CARD

The address only to be written here.

Write here for INLAND POSTAGE only.

Miss Dorothy Taylor
11. York Road.
Bury St. Edmunds

This is a rare postcard with the Thorpe postmark. Most of the post was stamped from the main Norwich office. This dates from 1903 which puts it into the newly extended no. 77 Yarmouth Road post office. The recipient was Miss Dorothy Taylor who was born in 1894, so was only nine at the time. Dorothy was at home in Bury St Edmunds with her father Fred, a Head Teacher, mum Catherine and her two brothers. The message from her cousin Kitty praises the view on the postcard of the Parkers Store and Thorpe Green

Thorpe Village & the Green

In 1969 the post office went public. The Act that made this possible was passed by Harold Wilson's Labour government, after three years of consideration. Labour believed a public post office would serve the needs of the consumer and operate more efficiently on the open market than a civil service department. Vaughan Read lived in the Thunder Lane post office for a large part of his life. He grew up there and then went onto run the place after his father retired. In 1995 Mr. Read said that the post office sometimes resembled a Citizens Advice Bureau. "Everybody expects us to provide them with answers to their problems" he said. He said that the post office was often a meeting place for many of the pensioners and was the only time they ventured out of their homes.

142 Thunder Lane today.

This journey started off with Caley Parker with his wagon and horse. To conclude the story it is only fitting to feature one of the youngest business men in Thorpe today. Neal Gurney became one the country's youngest sub postmasters when he took on the role at Thunder Lane Post Office at the age of 21. Neal attended local schools and has lived in Thorpe St Andrew all of his life. His father, Denver, bought the post office about twelve years previously, and had employed Neal as a counter clerk. By the time of a refit and relaunch in February 2013, Neal was the sub postmaster. This was made possible with the help of a national three-year investment programme by the Post Office in at least half of its current network. By May of the same year this branch was able to be included in the current account service being offered by the Bank of Ireland UK which was launched in twenty six branches. Neal won the Best Centrally Supported Branch in 2014.

By 2014 Neal had also taken over two other post offices in Harleston and Acle. The Thunder Lane shop stocks a large variety of goods from greetings cards to, car tax, gifts and a phone booth. Neal has also taken the step of being a coach to other sub postmasters and has an online coaching website which covers all areas of the post office including marketing, team coaching and public speaking. His post office now deals in all aspects of modern like and the World Wide Web is at the core of many of the services available. Some of the more up to date services include travel money, travel insurance, passport checks, travel apps and many more web based apps.

PICTURE CREDITS

BIBLIOGRAPHY

BANGER, J, NORWICH AT WAR (NORWICH, 1984).

BENSLEY. L, THE VILLAGE SHOP, (OXFORD, 2008).

EVANS. B AND LAWSON. A, A NATION OF SHOPKEEPERS, (LONDON, 1981).

HAVENLAND. G. NATION OF SHOPKEEPERS, (PLYMOUTH, 1970).

THORPE ST ANDREW PARISH LIFE MAGAZINE.

SNELLING. S NORWICH, A SHATTERED CITY, (SOMERSET, 2012).

VIVIENNE ROBERTS SCRAPBOOKS, C/O THORPE HISTORY GROUP.